D1740080

the
mute swan

the mute swan

john fair

The Gavin Press

First Edition 1985

© 1985 John Fair

All rights reserved. No part of this publication may be reproduced, stored in a retrieval system, or transmitted, in any form or by any means, electronic, mechanical, photocopying, recording or otherwise, without the prior permission of the publisher.

British Library Cataloguing in Publication Data

Fair, John
   The mute swan.
   1.   Swans
   I.   Title
   598.4'1   QL696.A52

   ISBN 0-905868-16-1
   ISBN 0-905868-17-X   Pbk

Published by The Gavin Press, Limington, Somerset, BA22 8EH

Printed in Great Britain by Castle Cary Press Ltd., High Street, Castle Cary, Somerset

Content

Illustrations

All the illustrations, except III and XVI, are original drawings by John Fair. 'The Pied Piper' was photographed by Mr. Brian Harding, and the Cygnet and Duckling by the author.

Introduction

This book is dedicated to the Fox-Strangways family who from 1543, and continuing to this day, have owned and maintained the unique nesting colony of Mute Swans at Abbotsbury in Dorset. They have also given shelter and sanctuary to hundreds of extra swans each winter on the Fleet, the eight mile shallow lagoon which lies behind the Chesil Bank on the coast of Dorset.

Sometimes these wintering numbers reach well over one thousand – in 1980 we had 1,238 Mute Swans on the Fleet for six months. Our actual resident herd hardly ever leave this piece of water, i.e. the Fleet, and numbers stay fairly constant.

Some of the wintering birds stay and nest with us in the spring, some pair with our birds, some never seem to breed, and others, after nesting for perhaps a year, have a rest. It is, however, fascinating running a colonial nesting herd. There has been a Swanherd at Abbotsbury since at least 1393. The name of the first Swanherd was William Squilor, and he was responsible to the owners of the Benedictine Order of the large Monastery at Abbotsbury. To-day I am responsible for the continued nesting of this colony of Mute Swans at Abbotsbury Swannery, to the family who have owned it since 1543.

John Fair, Swanherd,
Abbotsbury Swannery, Dorset
August 1985

Mute Swans

Mute Swan *Cygnus olor* **Why Mute Swan?**
The short answer is that this particular species have quieter vocal communications than the other seven species of swan in the world. However, one has only to be near a number of these birds to realise that they are anything but mute, have quite a large vocabulary, and this connected with posturing, i.e. movements and displays, adds up to a considerable language. This language is what this book is all about.

Swans

Mute Swan

Cygnus olor Order Anseriformes – family anatidae. One of the eight swans in the world. Mute Swans winter in Britain and are present all the year round.

Whooper Swan

Cygnus cygnus Winters in Britain, breeds in Russia.

Bewick Swan

Cygnus columbianus bewickii Winters in Britain, breeds in Russia.

Whistling Swan

Cygnus columbianus columbianus North American.

Trumpeter Swan

Cygnus cygnus buccinator Rarest of the swans, North American.

Australian Black Swan

Cygnus atratus There was a black swan in New Zealand similar to the Australian swan, but it is now extinct. The Black Swan is a colonial nesting species while in Australia. There is also a very small induced colony of Mute Swans in Australia.

Black Necked Swan

Cygnus melanocoryphus South American.

Coscoroba Swan

Coscoroba coscoroba More gooselike.

There is one other peculiarity which at one time was thought to be a separate species, and that is the Polish Swan. So called because up to fairly recent times some pinkish grey legged swans were sent to London markets as food from the Baltic regions, i.e Poland, hence the name 'Polish'. In all other ways they are identical to Mute Swans. We had an adult several years ago bearing all the hallmarks of a Polish Swan. The cygnets are hatched all white, not grey, with pink bill and legs, and the adults have pinkish grey legs with normal coloured bills.

2 The Mute Swan

The country of origin of Mute Swans is not known and shrouded in our historical past. It is also not clear how they arrived in the British Isles. At first it was thought that Richard the First brought a few back from Cyprus after the Crusades, but then Richard only just managed to return himself! Bones have been found in East Anglia dating back much earlier. Anyway, swans were certainly in Great Britain by the eleventh century. I have recently received a request for a radius wing bone from the lower wing, to reproduce an eleventh century flute. It is not clear whether the first domestic herds were started from wild pairs, or started straight away from introduced birds. Probably the pairs we see holding territories today are descended from domestic herds. The exception is at Abbotsbury where the management is very similar to what it was in the fourteenth century, except that the end product is not eaten, and is the only remaining managed 'Herd' in the world, as well as being the only nesting colony in the British Isles.

Domestic herds were quite numerous in the middle ages as, before the twelfth century, anyone could keep swans. After years of lax laws marking became legal in the fifteenth century. As the bird could only be kept by royal charter, with all the owners having their own marks, it became a prestige bird. It looked very beautiful, as well as decorative, and at that time, before the introduction of the turkey, was prized for food. The marks and laws were both complicated and involved. It is not the intention of this book to go into this aspect too deeply as there is a very good book on the subject, which you will find mentioned under 'Further Reading' in the back of this book. However, there were some nine hundred different 'Swan marks' by the reign of Queen Elizabeth the First, made either with a small branding iron or knife on the bill, or foot and heel. Today, as far as I know, there are only two areas where swans are still allowed to be marked, that is at Abbotsbury and on the Thames. There may be one or two marks in East Anglia. These days the Queen's swans are not marked in any way, so that all swans that are not marked and live on open waters such as rivers, canals, reservoirs, or any non-privately owned water, belong to the Queen. The Queen's Swanmaster and the Vintners' and Dyers' companies still have the 'Swan-upping' ceremony on the Thames each year during the swans' 'Moult', i.e. flightless period in July. The birds are herded by skiffs, caught, and the cygnets apportioned according to seniority. Firstly the Queen, then the Vintners' Company as they are the senior company, and the Dyers' Company. The Queen's being left unmarked, Vintners' cygnets are marked with two nicks with a knife on the bill, and Dyers' one nick on the bill. Sadly, partly due to fishing lead poisoning, not many pairs nest on the Thames these days. At Abbotsbury we still mark with a nick on the outside of each web, usually at the small cygnet stage. This is called the 'Hive of Ilchester'. Sometimes I leave this until the young are larger. This does not harm the bird, but there are a

Origin and History

Swan Marks

Swan-Upping
Moult

lot of small veins in a swan's foot and we avoid nicking these. This nick can be seen in the painting of the group of cygnets. The nick does not remain as a small cut in the web, but becomes a V-shaped depression in the older bird.

General Information

Swans do not 'sing before they die'. This is a myth and a reference to a politician who the author thought should die before he pontificated. Hence the quote: 'Swans sing before they die – 'twere no bad thing Did certain persons die before they sing.' (Samuel Taylor Coleridge – *Epigram on a Volunteer Singer*)

Size

Size – 5 ft. long.

Weight

Weight – Pen (Female) 18 – 25 lbs. Cob (Male) 20 – 42 lbs. These measurements are for birds which I have weighed myself over the years and give some idea how they can vary. The names Cob and Pen are only given to adult breeding birds. The origin of these two names is obscure.

Wing Span

Wing span – 6 ft. – 7 ft. 10 ins.

Flying Speed

Flying Speed – It has been calculated that with a tail wind, the mute swan can fly up to 60 m.p.h. although 20 – 30 m.p.h. is a more normal speed. All I know is that I have been doing 50 m.p.h. in a car and have been overtaken by a swan flying parallel.

Age

Age of Birds

Often birds are quoted at fifty years old. Unfortunately this age is an exaggeration and this seeming longevity is probably explained by the nest positions, which can be occupied by different birds over a period of many hundreds of years, merely because it is in a position which suits all swans. A large number of pairs have coloured rings these days and can be identified, so it is possible to tell how long the same pairs use the same nesting site. Many Mute Swans live to three years, a few to twenty-five.

Why aren't they camouflaged as other birds?

The Mute Swan is large enough and strong enough to look after itself. Juveniles on their own, old, and sick birds are generally speaking fair game for the fox, or fall foul of dogs. However, if in good health and on their own, they will depart the danger zone. Adults if defending a territory, or with young which cannot get away from the danger will attack with great courage and can, if they clout you with the correct part of the wing, break an arm or leg, but more about this in 'Nest and young defence'.

Because of the size and power of the adults they had no need to evolve with camouflaged plumage like our Mallard. This white plumage in scientific terms is called 'Continuous Advertisement', as wherever they are they are conspicuous. The cygnets light greyish brown down on the top merges with the colour of the water and gives them some camouflage from avian predators, while the beautiful pale silvery grey underside aids camouflage from such predators as pike looking up through the water. The mottled plumage of older young helps to break up the outline of the bird. During the winter young swans are difficult to pick out at a distance, as we know to our cost when counting them during the winter. Perhaps they all originated from more Northern climes where their white plumage would merge with snowy conditions and the juveniles' plumage with the mottled effect would be superbly camouflaged in tundra conditions?

Identification of the Male and Female breeding pair and young

The male is called a Cob and the female a Pen. Small young are called Cygnets, older young are often referred to as 'Siblings' or 'Blue-bills', as for much of the first year the bill is bluish-grey. However, usually all the young are called juveniles up to the first moult. Early in the breeding season, late January and February, the bill colouring of a breeding pair are similar, bright scarlet. When the female has laid eggs, the colour of her bill is much paler – see Illustration 1. Also at this time the cob's knob, or to give it its correct name 'Berry', is much larger than the female's. The term 'Berry' is because on closer examination it resembles a large black gooseberry with small white bristles over most of it. The purpose of this berry is not fully understood, but probably denotes some hormone activity, and certainly registers aggression. Its composition and consistency is rather like rubbery cheese. February, March, April, May, June and July the cob's berry is definitely larger than the female's and generally he is the larger bird. Part of August and September the female's role is slightly changed as she takes over the male's role of protection for the young whilst the cob moults. From August onwards identification can be a problem, especially if one is dealing with a large female and a smallish male. As already mentioned, up to August the male's role is defence of territory. However, in common with all birds he

Why are they White?

Continuous Advertisement

Identifying Male, Female

Blue-bills

Berry on Bill

Illustration I
Heads of a Cob, Pen and Cygnet.

Protection of Young
During the Moult

must moult, i.e. get rid of his old worn-out feathers. Waterfowl become flightless during the moult. If both birds of a pair with young were to do this simultaneously then there would be no defence for the young. The moult takes about six weeks and for practically all this time the bird is flightless, as among the first feathers to fall out are the flight feathers, i.e. primaries and secondaries.

During the period when the male moults, i.e. early August and early September, the pen, already having moulted, will take over the role of main protector of the territory and young. During this time the berry on her bill increases in size and the cob's usually decreases and her berry can, in some cases, at this time exceed the size of that of the cob. I have recorded this change in some fifty breeding pairs in the last four years, both Abbotsbury swans and incoming breeders alike, and in both colonial and territorial pairs. This at times can make identification difficult.

The adults' ability when caring for the young to spread this moult over a long period, with only one of the pair moulting at a time, so that one is always able to fly, is to me a wonderful adaptation. Moulting for pairs with young is later than with non-breeding birds, consequently this is a very dangerous time for any moulting non-breeder which should stray into the territory of a pair with young. I have only experienced two pairs in the last ten years from one hundred successful breeding pairs with young who have not arranged this moult properly.

Another method of identification on land, but again you need to have at least two together for identification comparison, are larger feet on the male. However, the one quick method to identifying the male from the female at any time of the year either on water or flying, is the length of the neck. So that even when one is trying to compare birds of similar size during the period when the pen has all her wing feathers fluffed up, and the male is moulting and consequently looking smaller, the neck of the male always appears longer. Knowing these factors makes it fairly easy to identify adults at any time of the year. This long neck can be seen in the second illustration – Illustration II. When birds are on the land and slightly apprehensive as this one is portrayed, they can extend this neck. 'Craning the neck' usually takes place before flight. There are more vertebrae in a swan's neck than a giraffe's and it has been said that it is the most flexible neck of any creature in the animal kingdom. The feet, as can be seen, are extremely large and help to make the bird very clumsy on land, and if they turn quickly they often tread on the other foot and stumble. The ankle joint is the one which appears to be where most people think the knee joint should be. It will also be noted that they have long nails. These nails on the feet can cause considerable damage both to the clothes and flesh when swans are being handled, as they tend to 'paddle' with their feet. However, owing to the size the feet are extremely efficient at propelling the bird at great

Illustration II
Head of a Mute Swan, Neck and Feet.

speed in the water. We call these feet 'Paddles', as of all the swan species the Mute Swan is first and foremost adapted to being on the water. They like to graze on grass but if compared with the Bewick Swan which walks well, rather gooselike in fact, then the Mute Swan is very clumsy indeed. In the past at Abbotsbury these 'paddles' were sometimes cut off dead birds and deboned and sewn together by past swanherds to make tobacco pouches. There is a flange on the inside of each foot and the scaly look gives a clue to their reptilean ancestry. The top sketch shows the bill and is a clue to feeding habits. It is serrated, not along the edge, but on the inside, both on the top and bottom mandible and the lower bill fits inside the top. The tongue which is long also is roof-shaped, and has sharpish points and a roughness all pointing backwards. This enables slippery plants to be gripped and plucked under water.

Bill Shape

In common with most birds except birds of prey, there is only one eyelid, at the bottom, plus a membrane which, when one gets close enough, is very much like a shutter on a camera. This flicks from the front to the back across the eye at a great speed and cleans the eye. The 'Nail' at the end of the beak is the black bit; it is also a good burrowing and gripping tool, and is used for placing the feathers in good order when preening. A most interesting point while talking about the head is that over the eyes are two desalination glands. Swans will live on brackish water as two or three food plants they particularly like grow in saline water. Salt is removed through the nostrils in concentrated liquid form, otherwise they would suffer from salt poisoning. They must have fresh water to drink however, so they always congregate round fresh water streams when living in brackish water or visit streams to drink at regular intervals.

Eyelid and Membrane over Eye

The Nail

Desalination Glands

The ears are also out of sight down on what we would term the cheek. Swans have good hearing and they also have good eyesight. It will be noticed, though, that when studying something the bird will be turning its head from side to side. The berry obscures sight to a certain extent in forward vision and, when flying, power lines are a real danger to them, causing many deaths. As I write this I am caring for a river cygnet which collided with power lines. Young birds probably cannot control their flight as well as adults.

The Ears

Power Lines

Identification of young birds is not so easy, i.e. birds about twelve months up to two years. The juvenile's whitish grey round its bill denotes age of roughly a bird about 5 to 6 months. The second winter the juvenile will be all white with a small berry, and will usually have a greyish red bill. These are immatures, which often I am asked about as they are in the company of several other birds of approximately the same age group and not associating with nesting pairs. When a swan has arrived on unfamiliar water he always shows 'Apprehension'. See Illustration IV. The top illustration is of a second year swan with a pale bill showing aggression as its wings are up, but poised for instant flight with neck craned.

Apprehension

Illustration III
'The Pied Piper' *John Fair feeding swans in the winter.*

'The Pied Piper'

The photograph was taken during a lull in the almost non-stop wet and very windy winter of 1982-1983, albeit comparatively mild. In the centre foreground there is just one cygnet. Only twelve from sixty-seven cygnets appeared to survive that winter, which was the worst survival rate I have experienced. To the left of the cygnet there is a swan with a 'wry' tail, i.e. permanently twisted to one side. This bird was some four years old, and I have never discovered whether or not this bird can fly.

The 'stained' look of these birds was created, I believe, by Fuller's earth, which is much in evidence in the Fleet when heavy and constant rain washes silt from the sloping land into the water. That, and competing in close proximity to one another, contributed to the dirty brown look, caused by worn feathers.

The combination of high water, too high to allow them to reach their natural foods, it is also very difficult for a swan to upend to reach food when a gale is blowing, and plant food shortages, resulted in something over a hundred birds perishing that winter. Some birds do not take kindly to being hand fed, not always incomers, sometimes our swans have a preference for natural plant food rather than hand fed wheat. They too have their food preferences, just like we do.

The middle two are typical attitudes, feathers 'sleeked', i.e. depressed, a sign of being unsure, with neck arched and head on one side.

'Sleeked' Feathers

The lower centre illustration shows slight aggression with the wings up, and the bottom two the same two birds 'shovelling' their bodies along in shallow water, feeding on corn, and in this case keeping a wary eye open for danger. Swans and cygnets will sometimes propel themselves along in very shallow water rather than walk. If you are near enough to a bird and you are not sure whether it is a bird in its second year, look for a triangular patch of brown feathers covered by the wings on the lower back, always the last feathers to turn white. This will denote a juvenile 9 – 12 months about to lose its last brown feathers. This can be seen if the bird 'upends' which enables a longer reach for the feeding bird.

Shovelling

Upending

Returning to juveniles, their wings do not have the whistle with which we associate the adult Mute Swans flying until they are about 6 – 7 months old. No one knows how this noise is made. The Whooper and Bewicks which winter in the British Isles do not have wings which 'whistle'. It is thought by scientists that this wing noise is used by Mute Swans to keep contact with one another at night in the absence of a loud vocal communication. I am not sure about this as even Mute Swans communicate vocally when flying, and can be heard calling to one another at a considerable distance away. We can call swans to us from over a quarter of a mile even when they cannot see us. So their hearing is quite good.

Whistling Wings

Illustration IV

Second and Third year Swans. The top swan is showing aggression, the middle two have their feathers sleeked, a sign of being unsure, and the lower centre swan shows slight aggression.

To keep the feathers in good condition much hard work has to take place and the sequence is as follows: daily, after feeding, bathing. Great enjoyment is evident here with much water splashing about, with often forward and sideways flips right over in the water. Next, the bird staggers ashore, shakes the bill to remove any debris, then a sideways motion down the front with the serrated side of the bill combs off excess water. The centre illustration of the next three shows the wings alternately flopping up and down to dry them and craning the neck and beating the wings forward, rather like the 'Triumph' posture, to remove excess water.

The right-hand illustrations show oil from the preen gland being rubbed by the chin to pass this oil right over the feathers. The nail on the bill all the time will be passed through to make the feathers lie the correct way – the left-hand illustration. This feeding, bathing, preening and sleeping sequence is essential to the bird's existence. Feathers fall into two categories, soft insulating feathers, and stiff flexible feathers. The latter play an important role in flight, i.e. wing and tail feathers. The preen gland consists of two small tufts of soft bristle-like hairs, yellowish, about ¼ inch long, over a 'pimple', i.e. a gland, which can exude this oil, and is situated on the lower back, properly called the 'lower rump'. The oil which is taken from it by the bird smells and feels rather like 3-in-one oil. The daily habit of taking the oil and passing it over the body by birds for waterproofing is in contention by scientists, as there is some evidence that vitamin D is released when the sun reaches the oil which has been spread over the body. However, I still subscribe to the waterproofing bit having been a trout fisherman for many years, and tied all sorts of feathers for fly fishing, both hard hackles and soft feathers, which sink very quickly if not oiled. Feathers have constantly to be re-oiled to make them float. Occasionally swans get impacted preen glands, and of course end up in a filthy state and die.

The last two illustrations on this page show the end of this sequence, i.e. sleep or what passes for sleep. Birds do not sleep in the same way as we do but 'catnap', i.e. one eye is opened at intervals to keep an eye on everything. Sleep, or 'roosting' to give it its correct name, takes place in most incredible positions but these are the two most usual, squatting down with bill tucked in the feathers and feet drawn up, or either standing on one leg, as this one is doing, or on two legs. Incidentally, most of these little illustrations were done from sketches in 1983 when I was feeding some three hundred birds twice a day during December, January and February and this bird had so much confidence in me that I was able to get within four feet of it, and it continued to sleep with its head away from me while poised on one leg.

Everyday Hygiene and Activity

Bathing

Preening

Preen Gland

Lower Rump

Impacted Preen Glands

Catnapping
Sleeping
Roosting

Illustration V
Bathing, Preening and Sleeping. The swans are shown, centre, removing excess water, right, oil from the preen gland being rubbed over the feathers, left, the nail being passed through the feathers, then catnapping.

Travelling in a Straight Line

Swans 'In-line'

Swans may be observed travelling in a straight line, one behind the other. I have seen forty-eight swimming in this fashion. It is probably derived from their youth, when this is the safest method to travel, i.e. one parent in front, one bringing up the rear and the juveniles in between. Adult swans usually only travel in this fashion when in the moult, or just coming out of the moult. 'Slip streaming' may come into this when juveniles travel behind an adult, but there is no change-over to enable the leader, who is taking the full brunt of the water turbulence, some respite when adults are swimming in this fashion.

Swimming Under Water

To escape a predator or escape from swan handlers who often use canoes or boats, adult swans will sometimes swim under water. I have only seen this once, when a moulting bird was trying to escape being drowned by a fiercely territorial cob. It was a very strange sight, a ghostly white shape paddling furiously for about twenty feet under water.

Illustration VI

These sketches of Mute Swans in typical attitudes show many of the daily routines and some reactions of the birds.

Key to Illustration VI

1, 2, 3 and 4, feeding in shallow water. 5, young swan, very unsure of itself, being aggressive, but moving from what it considers a danger area. 6, catnapping. 7, apprehension. 8, busking. 9, unsure of the closeness of humans. 10 and 11, aggression. 12, wing drying after bathing. 13, pen, moving away from danger area quickly, with very young cygnets on her back. 14, flight.

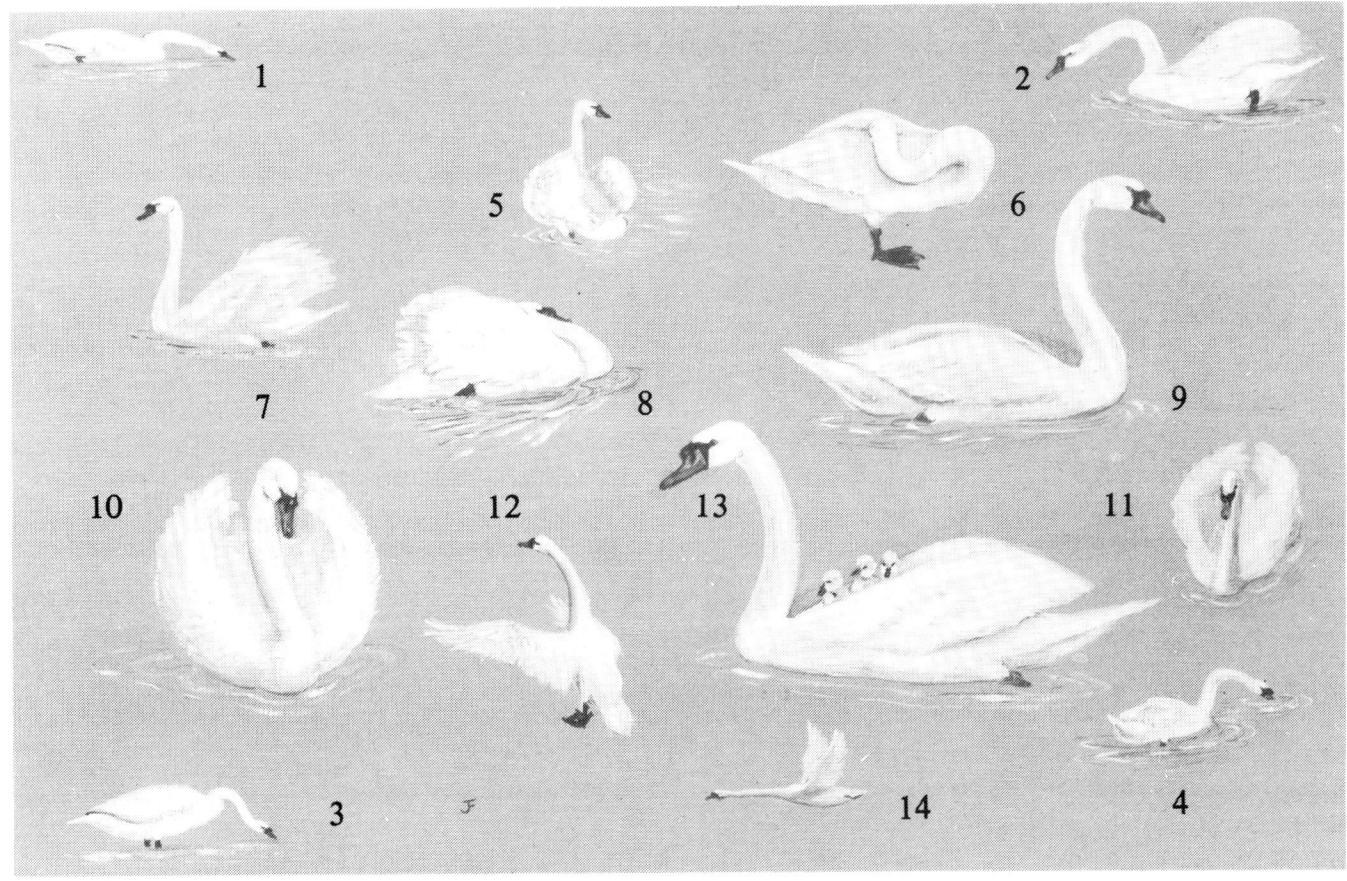

Courtship

'Pair Bond'

Average Age

Territory

Illustration VII
'Morning Flight' *This is a painting of the Western Fleet looking eastwards to Portland, with a pair of Mute Swans flying in to land on the Fleet during 'Courtship Flights'. A flight of Widgeon are winging their way back onto the Fleet after resting out in Lyme Bay, which they do fairly frequently.*

Courtship Flight

Courtship

This is the most interesting and involved sequence. Mute Swans are sexually mature at two years, but do not usually breed until 3, or more usually 4, years old. Courtship, however, starts at one year old, and we often have several young birds standing on our nesting site at Abbotsbury nodding away and making a heart shape with their necks, first to one then another. This head turning and staring is not fully understood but probably has something to do with identification. Is it possible this revolving of heads and gazing hard at each other's head is the pair trying to register the black area round the nostrils, as each shape is unique? These shapes vary only slightly and cannot be used for individual identification by humans as the black and yellow can be in Bewick Swans. The 'pair bond', the scientific term given to a pair which are firmly committed to one another, can happen at two years, but usually at three. It is a commonly held belief that swans mate for life and that they will only have one partner. This is more true of wild geese than swans, and when one of a pair of breeding geese has been shot or dies it is unlikely that he will find another mate. What does happen, however, with swans is this. People often say to me that one of their pair of swans at home has had an accident and that the other bird moped, pined and eventually died. The average age for a river, lake or canal pair is about eleven years and what is more likely is that both birds have died of old age. The size of the territory marked out and held by a cob is determined by how aggresive he is, and this varies considerably, depending on how much food is available. If submerged plant foods are sparse then a larger territory will be necessary.

The larger the territory the less likelihood of another bird entering that territory, so the remaining swan of that pair has less chance of finding a new mate. However, old birds do accept and mate with new partners. The best example I know of this was a twenty-four year old cob owned by the Marquess of Bath, the original pair having come from Abbotsbury. The pen died first which is fairly unusual, as in my experience females generally speaking, barring accident, live longer than males. We introduced another younger female who had a cygnet with her and had lost her mate. The old cob accepted the bird and the cygnet very readily, and she nested and laid eggs. Unfortunately she was killed by vandals, but the old cob also accepted another bird after the death of his second mate. All are individuals and will react differently and some may not accept a new mate, so there are no hard and fast rules.

A painting of a pair of courting swans on the Fleet in February about to circle prior to landing. The male behind the female has a slightly larger head and, as already mentioned, a longer neck. In flight swans' wings are extremely rigid, appearing inflexible, and only the primary, the large feathers on the ends of the wing, seem to move; this is not the case, however. When gliding in to land the wings bend at the 'wrist' bone considerably and the tail is spread. The feet are always kept in a streamlined position when flying except on landing when held forward as skids, or pattering on top of the water. I have seen only once feet used as tailplanes by three swans landing in a gale, when suddenly they were caught in a wind which threatened to dash them down, and most incredibly the 'paddles' were yanked upwards and flat above the body to give lift. This flying in the early spring and late winter is an essential part of courtship and continues in February, March and April. Often five or six birds together with the young of the year join in the courtship flights in our area.

Wrist Bone

Early courtship has already been mentioned and the 'pair bond', i.e. the strengthening of the determination to carry out successful nesting, consists of flight and gazing into each other's faces. This takes place on land and in the water. The second illustration shows this on water. As already mentioned, a 'territory', or area, will have been marked out by the cob and will be an area which he thinks will have a good safe nesting place with abundance of submerged plant foods which they can reach, i.e. not more than three feet and preferably 1 ft. 6 ins. to 2 ft. down. Often this territory is maintained throughout the winter, but this depends whether there is enough food for the winter. Swans will not often be found in very fast rivers where there is little plant growth. This illustration is of a young incoming pair to the Fleet, probably three years old, who stayed on into the winter on the outside of the herd, having arrived in December. The red stain on the head is caused by birds feeding in mud where much iron is present and always easily picks out 'foreigners' for us as there is iron present in our water but it never seems to affect or stain our birds' heads. The sequence in the top illustration was slight apprehension. Feathers 'sleeked', heads depressed, and the lower neck depressed into the water and tails made into a 'pinshape' by two birds not quite sure of one another, followed by proper courtship, necks fluffed, feathers raised like aggression, heads turning, and necks making a heart shape. This can take place on land as well as in the water and then follows head bobbing up and down in the water with feathers arranging with the bill (not shown) and then mating. This looks as if the female is being drowned as she is pushed down into the water, with the male gripping feathers at the back of her neck. The post mating sequence is strange. By bodies touching and feathers 'sleeked' again and much paddling they rear out of the water. This is accompanied by a peculiar and rather eerie moaning sound. Courtship can take place all the year round, so can mating. In fact swans mate far more often than would be required to produce eggs.

'Pair Bond'

Territory

Apprehension

Illustration VIII
Swans Courtship, Discoloured Heads. A young incoming pair of Mute Swans on the Fleet.

At this point I intend to differentiate between what I term 'territorial nesters' and 'colonial nesters'. These are the same species but in 'territorial nesters' there will be only two birds present in a given territory which will be extremely aggressive to other swans, humans and dogs, and sometimes all other waterfowl which enter their domain, as in their minds all these constitute a threat to their territory. 'Colonial nesters', as some at Abbotsbury, are not so aggressive, and much of the aggressive behaviour is tempered with 'ritualized behaviour'. Obviously they could not nest close to one another if this was not the case. This aggressiveness varies from pair to pair and I always think it interesting at Abbotsbury having one or two very aggressive pairs which nest 'territorially' each year as this makes a good comparison with our colonial nesting herd. The tell-tale signs of aggression are first and foremost the wings held erect and in the early stage the cob may just cruise up and down to you, head held high. However, when the territory is established all you will see of an attacking bird is a 'roof' of ruffled feathers. The cob and the pen will attack in this manner, the head is held right back in the ruff and tail held flat on the water. Propulsion is made by the bird scooping both feet together into the water; considerable speed can be attained in this way. The proper term for this is 'Busking'. All non-breeding swans will flee before this as they recognise the signal, but occasionally two breeding cobs of equal resolve meet and then a very spectatcular fight takes place with birds hitting out with the wrist bone on the wing, i.e. the bony bit halfway along. Blows are struck with one wing at a time, not both wings, and this is done with great speed. They will fight on land, in the air and on water. Fights to the death can sometimes take place over a suitable territory by equally matched contestants and the victor will grab his adversary's head, who has been battered and considerably weakened, and drown him. It is possible to successfully save cobs in these fights to the death, and I have done so twice. If one can get close enough it is not too difficult to haul off the winning bird as they are completely engrossed in what they are doing, but I would not advise the uninitiated to try to do so. These fights can continue for a day or two. However, any adult non-breeding birds which are moulting, flightless, and happen to stray into the territory of a family, are at a complete disadvantage and most certainly will be drowned. This happened with us in 1983 and again this year, 1985. I saw it happen but was unable to get to a boat and rescue the moulting birds in time. Their lungs are not very large. One good territorial cob can keep literally hundreds of moulting birds out of his territory.

The bottom illustration shows a pen carrying young on her back for safety. In this case the bird has been on land and is 'shovelling' off into the water while the cob goes into attack. Very few waterfowl carry young on their backs. The young nearly always climb up on the leg, rarely from the front, and

Territorial and Colonial Nesters

Roof

Busking

Wrist Bone

Illustration IX
Cob Busking, Pen with Cygnets on her back. Aggression and a mother taking her young to safety.

Adults Carrying Young

in fact are shaken off if they try. Mergansers carry their young and so do Great Crested Grebes.

Criteria for Choosing a Nest Site

(1) Shallow water not over three feet in depth.

(2) Relative peace and quiet. Swans do not like being harried by sailing boats. Rowing boats, except of course 'racing' rowing boats, they can cope with. The most disastrous boat to them however is the new menace to many waterfowl on large waters in this country, the sail board. These sail boards travel at such speed that birds cannot get out of the way quickly enough. Motorboats can also be a menace to them, although swans can often be seen hanging around boats for 'hand-outs' of food.

(3) Abundance of food under the water.

(4) Reed leaves are often pulled and young leaves eaten, and to this end swans can help to keep back the complete colonization of reed beds which can obliterate large areas of fresh water in a very short time.

(5) Reed or similar plants for nest-making. The area may be a canal, river or a large lake or a small pond, an estuary, or as in our case on the Fleet, an eight mile saline lagoon.

Plant Foods

Fresh Water: (1) Potamogeton species
           (2) Algaes – of many species
           (3) Canadian Pondweed
           (4) Water Crowfoot
           (5) Reed
           (6) Roots of water plants
           (7) Watercress
           (8) Fools cress

Salt Water: (1) Eel grass species (a flowering grasslike seaweed)
           (2) Ruppia-Wigeon grass, and Algaes
           (3) Ulva Lactuca – Sea Lettuce
           (4) Enteromorpha species
           (5) Algaes of varying kinds

Swans have been recorded as eating dead fish but only when starving as they are 98% vegetarian. Some small crustaceans get eaten with the plant food.

The Nest

When the territory has been marked and maintained by the cob the nest site is chosen mutually, and not entirely by the cob as some authorities suggest. The nest can be a very large construction, added to year after year. Swans can sense rising water and will try to raise the nest at times of imminent flooding, but are usually caught out with flash flooding. They do not fly and carry nesting material as do our garden birds, but make use of any material within forty feet, but more

Criteria for Choosing a Nest Site

Plant Foods

Fresh Water

Salt Water

Illustration X
Two Swans, Necks forming a Heart Shape. The bright scarlet bills are indicative of a breeding pair during late winter into spring, the necks forming a heart shape, which is a typical courtship attitude.

The Nest

usually up to twenty feet. They even use plastic containers in some of our cities, a terrible indictment of the twentieth century. We always place extra material near nests when we are going to get Spring tides and the swans tuck it in very quickly. In this connection I believe they can detect changes in the barometer, i.e. high and low pressure. Generally speaking the nest is the shape in Illustration XII, built by both the pen and the cob, and gradually grows. Birds sometimes sit side by side on the nest reaching for pieces of material and pass this to one side or the other, or, more usually, the cob works material gradually back to the nest, then it is tucked into the correct place by the female. The sloping sides are no accident, and enable eggs which inadvertently fall out to be worked back up again into the nest by putting the bill over the egg and rolling it up with the underside of the bill. I have, however, never seen this happen at Abbotsbury, and eggs outside a nest usually stay there. This sloping side also enables cygnets, which sometimes fall out in the first day or when returning to the nest, to clamber back up again. I have seen this many times, as small cygnets have very sharp claws and by flattening themselves can keep their centre of gravity low, enabling them with these sharp, curved claws and tiny wings out for balance, to climb quite steep slopes. Only small amounts of down are placed into the nest plucked by the female from her own body.

Illustration XI
The Egg. This painting shows the actual size of a Mute Swan's egg.

Eggs

Eggs vary from 4 ins. by 2½ ins. to 5 ins. by 3 ins. and are elliptical rather than hen-shaped, have very thick shells and are bluish-grey, which eventually become olive-coloured when polished by the pen turning them in the nest. The number laid varies from one to twelve, but the average is six eggs. The complete number is called a 'clutch'. Occasionally very tiny eggs are laid. I have two records of this out of several hundred breeding pairs of swans during the past ten years. One was completely round, and the size of one of those large marbles we used to play with, and the other egg was bantam, or sub-standard size. The tiny eggs are the first ones of the season and, of course, do not hatch. Normal sized eggs weigh approximately ¾ lb. Only one clutch is laid per year, although occasionally, if the first clutch is destroyed, swans will lay again. This year, 1985, we have had two pairs of swans who laid seven eggs and six eggs in their individual nests. These were subjected to flooding on two consecutive days. The eggs were under water for six hours on each day. After sitting for some time when the tide had subsided, they realised that the eggs were not developing and deserted the nests for approximately ten days. One morning we suddenly realised that there were three extra eggs in each nest, which eventually hatched. We removed the addled eggs before hatching. The colour of the later eggs was more blue, and they retained heat and had no smell.

The Egg

The Egg of the Mute Swan

Every Mute Swan lays a unique shaped egg, as of course do all other birds. They are all elliptical, and not wider at one end than the other. There is, however, considerable variation; some are long and slim, others fatter. This one is a typical shape and a good size.

On hatching, the egg is very pale and chalky blue green. After being rolled about in the nest by the swans at the 'changeover ceremony', i.e. the male or female coming to take a turn on the nest, the eggs become polished and more olive in colour. When first laid, scratches appear through the chalky substance; these are made by the swan's own claws, which are quite formidable.

The gradual deepening from blue to olive enables us to determine in a clutch which egg was the last one to be laid. It also enables us to determine whether the nest is regularly occupied or not.

If the cygnets are lost no replacements are laid again that year. The females normally lay one egg every other day but I have noticed with my records that if the bird is in a hurry, or late nesting, she will lay one every day. Very often, with experienced birds, they will bury the first egg quite a long way down in the nest; sometimes this is forgotten, but more usually brought up and incubated with the rest of the 'clutch'. Again 'incubating', i.e. the placing of the correct body heat by exposing a 'brood patch', or bare flesh, by the female on to the eggs, does not normally take place until the clutch is complete, so that all the cygnets hatch within a day or two of each other.

Incubating
Brood Patch

The early stages of clutch completion is the vulnerable stage for egg disappearance. The nest is left unattended for some of the time as twenty-four days can elapse between the laying of the first egg to the female being properly committed to incubation – as already stated twelve eggs are possible, laid at two days intervals. During this time the female will join the male on the water where mating takes place, feeding and generally looking after the water territory, the land territory being quite small. The eggs take about thirty-five days to develop, and incubation does not normally start until the last egg is laid. All this time while sitting, the eggs will be turned at intervals. No one has yet really discovered fully the reason why hatching eggs have to be turned, possibly to keep the developing embryo free and to stop it becoming gummed up in the egg. The Wildfowl Trust have been doing experiments on this during the last few years with goose eggs. I have recorded several pens who have laid an egg up to a week after incubation has started. This egg does not often hatch, but again, I have three records in the last ten years when a 'ticking' egg has been left in the nest. The ticking, which is quite audible, is the cygnet breathing and sounds much like a tiny timebomb. This ticking happens just before hatching when the cygnet has broken through the membrane and gulps air from the air sac. We always pick up these eggs and check for this ticking after the family have left, and if the embryo is still alive, give it to another bird whose eggs are about to hatch. I must mention here that it is illegal to do this with swans, and this is discussed in a later episode headed 'The Law'. Only with scientists who have licences or birds privately owned is this permissible.

Nest Relief

Nest Relief Ceremony

The cob at nesting time relieves the pen at the nest to give her a chance to drink and to stretch her legs. During the time when one of a pair is arriving to relieve its partner at a nest, a ceremony, rather quiet and easily overlooked, takes place. This consists of the two birds producing the 'head lift', a sign of recognition. This is usually accompanied by a low vocal sound. After a moment or two the bird being relieved walks off the nest, or often slides down the side of the nest, and while doing this invariably takes a small amount of nesting

Head Lift

Egg Predation

material from the ground and tucks it into the nest before leaving.

Now apart from human vandalism of nests, foxes, having once tasted swans' eggs are very partial to them, especially a vixen with cubs when her young are small. We frequently find eggs half buried which have been carried sideways, with teeth marks arranged in the correct place for a fox mouth. We have also experienced one year an extremely clever vixen, who visited our nest site and had thirty-six eggs from different nests, all to feed very young cubs. The eggs have a high protein content which is good for the young cubs before they are fed rabbits. This happens practically every year, and is on record for many past years for us. Dogs also seem partial to swans' eggs, and we have several records of this from different parts of the country. We have also had a mink, we believe, taking eggs this year, 1985, and have found sizeable chunks bitten in the top, and the egg sucked out, quite different to the positioning of fox teeth marks, which we also find on eggs when the fox has been disturbed when egg stealing.

Nest Defence

This illustration shows what happens with the pen on the nest. Hissing, wings dropped, exposing the 'wrist bone' prior to standing up on the eggs, the eggs can take the full weight of the cob, ready to deliver blows to the fox. I have witnessed a fox attack on a nest twice. On both occasions only one bird was present, the female, and on both occasions the female was quite capable of driving off the fox – this was in 1975 and 1980. It cannot be that Abbotsbury is the only place where foxes take eggs. The sequence here shows the pen being aggressive and leaving the warding off of the attack to the cob. As can be seen the cob's neck is fluffed and he is hissing very loudly to warn off the danger. He has reared up, two legs braced and the tail dug in to make a tripod and a better stance. The blow is delivered with one wing, not two, and if the fox is in range he could be killed with one of these extremely fast, well-aimed blows, though this is unlikely.

The final illustration shows 'Triumph'. The enemy has been driven off and the cob rears up, beats his wings with vigour, and produced a descending vocal snort, with eyes staring, and gradual lowering of the neck. This 'Triumph' is also shown when a human enters a territory and leaves again. We have on record an alsatian dog, when attacking a nest, being killed, but it is also on record that an alsatian dog has killed nesting swans. Nesting pairs before the thirteenth century, remember, had to contend with wolves at times, and that might be one of the reasons for our nesting colony, i.e. defence in numbers. They must have been able to deal with wolves or they would not have survived as a successful British nesting species. I can still remember those two fox strikes very clearly, and they both started with the fox just standing and sizing up the situation quite close. I was so fascinated that I watched it for a long time, especially on the second occasion. After sizing up the situation the fox circled the nest, eventually running quite fast, with the pen turning and hissing with wings up and feet covering the eggs. If the pen had got off the nest to attack the fox then the faster and more intelligent creature would have nipped in and taken an egg. In this nest defence I have been given many instances of young humans, when attempting to take eggs, who have been badly knocked about, and received broken arms and collar-bones. I also know of handlers who were doing scientific work who have had broken bones. These accidents are often caused by the cob who, if in the water, 'busks' across, as already described, and when reaching the nest will be flying into the attack. Then the sequence is complete. One of my colleagues was knocked head-over-heels in one of these attacks.

Nest Defence

Triumph

Illustration XII
Cob and Pen Defending Eggs against a Fox, Triumph. The male reared up, legs braced and tail dug in to make a tripod. The enemy is driven off, then Triumph.

Busking

Cygnets

A look at cygnets will give a clue as to why swans are so aggressive in their defence. Cygnets do not have the ability to dive any distance under water at one or two days old, or swim under the water for fifty yards, or even further, as do shelducklings for example, although they can dive under, but bob up rather quickly. Wing development in the young cygnets is extremely slow, making them very vulnerable for a long time. But which came first, the aggressiveness of adults to protect the young, or has the development of the cygnet become slow because there is no hurry, as in ducks, to reach maturity because the young have adequate protection? This one I often ponder. When cygnets are much older they can swim considerable distances under water.

Cygnets on hatching are able to walk about, albeit in a wobbly fashion, within twelve hours of hatching. This almost self-supporting ability is called 'precocial', i.e. very precocious as opposed to 'altricial', or completely dependent on being fed, such as young Blackbirds.

All waterfowl, Pheasants and Partridges, in fact all ground nesting birds, produce precocial young.

Imprinting

Imprinting is the acceptance of the correct parent by the cygnet. About three days or so before hatching the developed cygnet takes it first breath from the air sac at the end of the egg. The ticking sound, i.e. breathing, as already mentioned, is very audible at this stage. The pen, who is always on the nest for hatching, will call to the cygnet with a call which sounds rather like a dog barking to imprint her voice on the young. In fact a pen when returning to a nest of eggs, even in the early stages of completing a clutch, will give her imprinting call to eggs. All swans have a similar call, used by cobs and pens alike. However, all calls are different in pitch. Some females have a squeaky, hardly audible call, whilst others have a really loud 'bark'. The young also have to learn to recognise the calls of their mother and father. This creates real problems for cygnet imprinting in a colony, but there is no such problem for 'territorial' young, and is the reason for rearing pens at Abbotsbury for some pairs.

On starting to hatch, which takes about twelve hours, the wet looking and bedraggled cygnet which emerges from the egg will see a large white object with black feet, so imprinting is partly sound and partly sight. Parents often stand on them, but this does not seem to hurt them.

The family take to the water usually a day after the last cygnet is hatched. The young are occasionally reluctant to enter the water at first, but with much calling mother persuades them in. All cygnets 'roll' from side to side when they first touch the water. I have never made up my mind whether this is a balance problem, or the shock of cold water on warm feet.

The pink 'nail' on the end of the bill, which later on in

Vulnerability of Cygnets

Precocial
Altricial

Imprinting Problems

Illustration XIII
In this painting of cygnets there is a typical number of five, just waking up and preening. They go through this process exactly like mother and father, although the cygnets have no preen oil in the preen gland at first. Note the pink nail, the position of the 'egg tooth' and a nick in the outer webb 'The Hive of Ilchester', our swan mark.

'Roll'

Egg Tooth

'Trill'

Comfort Movements

Foot Paddle

adults becomes black, is where the 'egg tooth', the small flattened thornlike hard piece used by the cygnet to chop its way out of the shell, can be seen in the cygnet painting. (Illustration XIII). This egg tooth is present for three to four days, and has certainly gone by one week old. If one can get close enough this is quite a good method to age a very small cygnet.

Cygnet calls are varied. They have a 'trill' similar to ducks when settling down comfortably. They have the same leg stretch movements and head movement of beak into their body down, accompanied by a little head shake called a 'comfort movement'. All swans have these comfort movements. Dogs have this little 'head shake' when they feel safe and contented before sleep. The cygnets have a hungry cheep, rather high pitched, and a very high pitched voice when lost. They are not fed by parents like Moorhen or Coot chicks, but will have to find food for themselves, but both parents will 'foot paddle' in water to swirl up exciting food items, and will pull reed leaves down, and bring up plants from deeper water and drop them near to the young. I have seen a cygnet at three days old standing in about 1 inch of water 'foot paddling' furiously. An instinctive foot paddle routine or, as mother has just been doing the same thing, had it been learned?

The Mute Swan does not immediately recognise its own young. As already mentioned we have problems with young constantly getting lost in our colony. This is not the fault of the parents, but a problem of imprinting. Remember it is the cygnet which has to imprint on the adults by both sight and sound. Regularly we have adults who have lost their young for one reason or another. Swans will continue to look for lost ones for up to a week, and this is quite heartbreaking to see. Last year, 1984, for instance, we had a pair who lost all their four cygnets. On arriving at our nesting area one morning six days later, we found three lost, wet, bedraggled and very cold young being harried badly by non-breeding adult swans, who sometimes will drown young. We gave the cygnets to this pair, who accepted them immediately as their own. This can usually only be done with cygnets up to a week old as there is little growth in the first week, and swans will, if they think the 'size' is wrong for their own young, reject them. Secondly, the cygnet after one week is imprinted on particular calls and will not accept any other swan. In fact if we gave a lost cygnet who is already imprinted to a pair with cygnets, even if the size of cygnet is just right, then the reaction of the young, i.e. swimming up and down 'piping' in a high pitched voice, **'Piping'** which means 'I am lost, come and find me', will mean that one or other of the parents will drown that cygnet.

In this context of imprinting adult swans, when fighting over maintaining the control of water territory, will do one of two things. The victors of the dispute will either take over the other cygnets, or, if they look to be the wrong size, often drown them. I have experienced a particularly broody female who started off with six young, and after a fortnight ended up with thirty-three young! The cygnets like to be together, and one small cygnet, if not already imprinted, will joyfully accept a family group. Family life appears to be partly the security of large, powerful birds, and partly the pleasure which cygnets obviously take in each others company.

Departures from Normal

Departures from Normal

There is usually a reason for what appears to us abnormal behaviour if we could understand it. This occurs only if something is wrong with one of the young and if the pen or cob have a cygnet they do not like the look of, usually a weakling. There are two methods for despatch of the young.
   (1) Drowning if the family is on the water, the more usual.
   (2) From the land the cygnets are either grabbed by the swan's bill and thrown about, or stamped on repeatedly until flattened. This is rare and, as already stated, there is a reason although we may not understand it. Swans are superb parents and guard their young well.

Growth of the young is very slow and unlike all other waterfowl the young take four and a half to five months before flying. Cygnets greet mother and father with the 'head **Head Lift** lift' and low sounds. Parents also greet one another and their young in this manner. People known to swans are also greeted by the swans and young with this recognition, which I believe does not mean 'I like you' but 'we recognise you'. In this context swans and quite young cygnets do not take long to recognise individual humans and both myself and my staff at Abbotsbury are identified by them. They recognise firstly clothes, i.e. gum boots or a particular hat, but then we often have visitors in similar clothing. The swans clinch the recognition with individual human voices. Now I base this on the following which I often demonstrate to prove the point. A complete change of clothing, say in the afternoon, followed by mixing with our visitors. This usually fools them. No problem until you talk. This brings instant recognition even from young cygnets. Perhaps swans recognise one another by voices?

Predation

Predators on Cygnets

The fox has already been mentioned as one of the predators both at the egg stage and for young cygnets. The rat, especially the bitch rat with young will, if she can, kill cygnets. Not so the water vole, the 'Ratty' of *The Wind in the Willows* fame, who is largely a vegetarian. Mink are an ever-increasing menace to all forms of wild life both great and small, and although attractive creatures should be dealt with quickly, as Water Rails, Moorhens, Coot, and particularly water voles, are affected. In fact all marsh and water abiding creatures are disastrously affected when mink appear.

Pike in fresh water pull cygnets down and the domestic dog can also be a danger. In our case with salt conditions, one of the predators is the Greater Black-backed Gull. Predators often play a part in picking off the young of creatures which depart from the normal behaviour patterns, consequently a better adapted population will result if the predation is not too widespread. We do intervene at times, but the secret in all conservation work is knowing when to leave well alone.

Juvenile Development

At about six weeks small brown areas of feathers begin to develop over where the wings are. This is kept pace by the tail feathers as shown in the illustration on page 35.

Elevated Legs

The elevated leg position is a typical attitude adopted by the young and adults, although very tiny cygnets cannot elevate their legs as shown in the second illustration down overleaf. Most people who have never studied swans think that the 'poor bird' who is carrying one of its legs either in this position or claw-like into its side or completely tucked into the soft side feathers, has a deformed leg. These three positions are completely normal. The scientific explanation is heat loss. The web has many veins practically on the surface and to keep them in cold water all the time makes them extremely cold. It is warmer out of the water than in, and Mute Swans often swim with one leg up for considerable periods and are completely mobile with one leg in this position.

The top illustration shows a juvenile September to October time, showing aggression. The gradation of light fawn for the primaries and secondaries down to a warmer brown is typical of juveniles changing from brown to white, a gradual process over the winter. I believe each pair of swans produce young which change their cygnet or sibling feathering to white plumage in a unique fashion, although all our young at Abbotsbury are very similar, with some however having light plumage. Incomers have different and much more blotched plumage. There will often be two such patterns to each pair, one following father and one following mother. One of our territorial pairs which has now been nesting with us for the past four years produce young whose white plumage pattern of development is the same each year, and I can pick them out from the other cygnets, even if the parents are not with them. Another example of this is a territorial pair on our decoy pond, who have nested in the same place for the last three years and are Abbotsbury bred birds, producing one young of each year's brood whose all-over fawnish-brown is considerably lighter than its brothers and sisters, in fact almost like a Whooper or Bewick juvenile.

The lower illustration shows 'upending'. Although swans use water up to one metre in depth when feeding, and can just reach plants at that depth when they upend, they expend considerable energy and, as already mentioned, one and a half feet to two feet is an ideal depth for feeding.

When the young can fly they are often driven away by their parents and drowned if they will not leave. This makes sense as the numbers over the years would build up, meaning there would be much competition for food in the guarded territory for themselves and young during that year, and eventual loss of food source. This varies enormously from pair to pair, however, as adults sometimes keep their young with them right up to the time the first egg is laid the next year. It really depends whether they migrate or not for the winter food. At this stage the juveniles are at great risk if driven away and have less chance of surviving than young taken by parents on to winter feeding areas.

Migration

The Mute Swan has no real migration like the Whooper and the Bewick Swan. This is fairly involved as part of the reason is the Mute Swan's status, i.e. they are neither tame nor wild but in between. In many places, judging by the number of telephone calls and letters I receive each year, some will not have to leave summer quarters to find winter quarters where there is abundance of food because someone is feeding them. Unfortunately much of the food given is bad for them; for instance white and ordinary brown bread is not very good, although it is better than nothing. Stale well soaked wholemeal bread is the best. Wheat fed in water is what we use in the winter, and is higher protein than maize.

If one takes away these 'fed' birds then there are basically

Cygnets from Down to Brown Feathers to Gradually Changing to White Plumage

Illustration XIV
Juvenile Aggression, Leg-up, Upending. The colouring is from light fawn to a warmer brown.

Upending

Young on Flying Sometimes Driven Away by Parents

Migration

Winter Migration

two migrations. A 'moult' migration when, before the birds become flightless, a very dangerous period in their lives, they must find a safe haven with abundance of food. This food might be waste grain from maltings, or a large natural area with abundance of plant food. This happens in late June and July. We have found that on the Fleet our 'herd' numbers are sometimes doubled and trebled, from July to August, by incoming birds from three counties, Somerset, Devon and other parts of Dorset. We are a vast safe piece of water with abundance of natural food which can be easily reached without coming on land. The Mute Swan is an opportunist and learned a long time ago that most humans are 'good news' so are often in close proximity to human habitation at moulting time.

The other migration is within the country for winter quarters and means flying along water ways to 'pastures new'. An estuary, alongside 'drowned' meadows, at the river side, or a large lake, anywhere their plant foods grow and can be reached. So although somewhere like Windermere has abundance of plant food, most of it is too deep for swans, so there will only be one or two pairs there. These winter migrations are only about fifty or sixty miles at the most. Only during extreme winters will these birds move over long distances. There are considerable numbers in Poland. These fine people have a great love of their swans now and protect them assiduously. In fact, even in Russia, the penalty for killing swans is one year's imprisonment. Russian swans winter in mid-Europe.

Mortality in Cygnets

When the cygnets are able to fly and have to find a new territory for themselves, mortality is high as already stated. They collide with power lines and even when there is a reasonable food source, they sometimes do not make it through their first year. If they can make the first winter then they have a good chance. This of course happens to all birds' young whether large or small. Only a small proportion of the young survive.

The most critical time in the first year for cygnet survival is during the second week of its life. There is enough food within the egg to keep the newly hatched cygnet going for the first week. If there is not ample food after this then it will die.

Swans' Association with other Waterfowl

When the Mute Swan is holding a breeding territory, and sometimes even when not, they can be extremely aggressive to other waterfowl, and will drown duckling. However, this varies from bird to bird and our swans at Abbotsbury usually live in close harmony with Mallard, and in the winter, when feeding on the lush *Zostera* beds, will have up to 10,000 Widgeon packing round them, benefiting from the swans' greater ability to reach food in deep waters. Swans tend to be rather wasteful feeders, and the resulting swathes of floating weed help the Widgeon considerably.

Moult Migration
Flightless

Association with
Other Wildfowl

Illustration XV

Mallard Duckling. An orphan, reared by the author. Mallards are often seen in close proximity to Mute Swans.

The Mallard Duckling

Swans and ducks often live in close proximity, and in many places live amicably. I have already mentioned the close association between Widgeon and our swans on the Fleet, particularly during high water, when the Widgeon are unable to reach the plant food. Sometimes, however, a breeding pair of Mute Swans who have Mallard in their chosen breeding territory can be very aggressive to other waterfowl, and will drown their ducklings. These other birds are regarded as a threat to the swan's food territory.

This Mallard duckling was brought to me many years ago, as all the rest of the family and mother had been killed crossing a road. We reared him to maturity and he survived for eight years, flying about to where he felt he wished to go. One day, in the autumn, he failed to return.

He had many adventures, at one stage he landed on a wet road at dusk thinking it was a river. Swans and ducks mistake very wet roads for rivers sometimes when the light is bad.

The Wells Swan

Two years ago I received a telephone call from a local police sergeant who has always been interested in birds, and is particularly good at resuscitating injured birds of prey. A cygnet, two or three days old, had been found stumbling down a road, in a town, all by itself, and taken to him. The cygnet was put with a Mallard duckling, and the two reared together. There came a stage in the rearing process when they had outgrown firstly a small bowl for bathing, and then the bath in the bathroom, which had been duly filled daily to enable these two young birds to carry out their washing and preening. It was at this stage that I was asked if I would continue the rearing process. These two small fellows were by this time inseparable friends, and naturally became upset if parted. I reared the two of them on a pond at home, but I was unwilling to release them into the wild owing to the cygnet not having enough body weight to take it over the initial stage of finding food for itself, or for that matter a long enough neck to reach that food.

We had already had a request from the Bishop of Bath and Wells for a pair of swans. The Moat at Wells has swans who ring a bell when they wish to be fed. The daughter of one of the bishops in the nineteenth century amused herself by training a swan to do this, and the tradition has been continued. The old pair had already been replaced by us the year before, but showed no sign of learning the art of bell

Illustration XVI
Cygnet and Duckling. Reared together, then taken to live on the Moat at Wells, Somerset.

ringing, then one died, so if the sex was right then the cygnet and duckling would be ideal for release on this water.

While we were rearing the cygnet and duckling in the garden they came to associate the ringing of a small bell with food time, and when we eventually took them to the Moat at Wells only three weeks passed before the cygnet had learned how to ring a bell to ask for food. Unfortunately the waterfowl collection kept by the Right Reverend John Bickersteth, Lord Bishop of Bath and Wells, on the Moat receive so much bread from the general public that it is rare for the swans to ring and ask to be fed these days.

Swans and Farming

Relations with Man

Although living on our canals, rivers and lakes without causing problems, they can at times, if in large numbers, produce problems to farming. I meet a lot of farmers who visit us from all over England and basically most of them accept that their fathers and grandfathers before them had swans grazing by the riverside during the winter on their land. Most people like having them around. Sometimes in December, January and February when other plant foods are hard to come by they can cause problems flattening the ground with their large feet and paddling the ground if they are in large numbers, but cropping a field can have the same effect as putting sheep into a lay to thicken and strengthen the planting.

However, there are a number of ways which can be tried to get them to leave, although swans can be stubborn at times. A low fence can prevent a 'walk on, walk off' situation which they particularly like, with streamers made from cutting up polythene bags tied on to long stakes. Large numbers of these will be required as, contrary to belief, Mute Swans, if they

Taking Off and Landing on Land

have a strong wind in the area, can take off with only a few steps and land in fairly small spaces. 20 to 30 paces between the stakes will help. Another method is intermittent bangers but this has a limited use. We employed a young lad as a bird 'scarer' one year, rather like they used to in bygone years, but the cheapest and most effective method we have discovered

Kite Balloons

so far are 'kite balloons' (made by Mr. Stewart of Stewkie Kites, Manor Farm, Melbury Osmund, Dorset) tied into a field, with the balloon about fifty feet up. These are not ordinary balloons but move about on a running line in a lively fashion as they have magnets inside and are quite large. To fit a rustling kite tail as well would keep most birds from a crop where real problems are being met. One must remember that these birds are going to someone else's patch if you drive them away, and by far the best thing in the long run is to try and get together with other landowners and your local N.C.C. representative and create an area where swans can go during the time of food shortages, where the crop is not immediately required. I personally gather as many swans

Feeding in Winter

together as I can for the last three months of the winter, the most vulnerable time, as we are talking about a large bird which requires a fair amount of food daily, and feed them wheat in water. I often end up with over half the Fleet population which relieves food supplies for other species as well as the remaining more nervous swans. A family or two could easily survive on stale wholemeal brown bread although their preference is always grass or some green stuff.

Helping Swans

Helping Swans
Young Driven Away

Having said all this there are times during the autumn when cygnets are driven away from a pair's territory and collide with obstacles and need help. No one is going to object to anyone trying to help in these circumstances. Or, as already mentioned, if flooding is present or imminent at nesting time Nest Flooding extra nesting material can sometimes make the difference between a successful nesting and all the eggs being washed away. (Although remember the cob is not going to understand your motives.) If one is dealing with an injured bird do not be inhibited by the hissing, the bite from a swan is not half as bad as that from a Canada Goose and does not really hurt, but wings should be immobilised quickly. The best thing to do, however, is to contact the R.S.P.C.A. who will usually help, but I am afraid this varies from place to place.

I well remember my first encounter with a pair of swans which were privately owned, where a young cob had been introduced on a small lake to an old pen who was well past breeding age. The young cob had the largest berry on his bill, bar one, that I have ever seen. The owner asked us if we would remove this bird for her as everyone in this small village when passing the pond had to take a stick or some instrument to ward off the young bird as he attacked everybody, and had even attacked cars. We duly arrived on a freezing cold day with our 'swan crook' and our large Swan Crook carrying crate. The 'swan crook', sometimes in some places called a 'swan pole', is what official swan handlers put round the neck of a bird prior to drawing it forward and immobilizing the wings. The crook looks like a shepherd's crook but with a smaller nape. Full of bounce and standing precariously on the edge of this fairly deep pond I stood with the crook poised. Sure enough the cob rushed across and went into the attack. I put the crook round his neck, he turned round and flew into the middle of the pond. Unfortunately I forgot to let go and ended up quite a considerable way out up to my armpits in freezing cold water. I then realised what powerful flyers they are. It gave considerable pleasure to the villagers, and considerable embarrassment to me. On another occasion a lady rang me up to say that a swan was sitting on a path at the side of the main road watching the traffic go by. She had given it some 'bread and milk'. It is surprising the number of people who think swans require milk. She asked us to come and do something before it caused an accident. I arrived with my 'swan crook', but unfortunately the swan decided 'discretion was the better part of valour', did not like the look of me, took off and flew straight and very low right up the middle of the road, over the heads of the holiday traffic. The expressions on the drivers' faces had to be seen to be believed. It all ended without any problems, however, as the traffic slowed up and stopped. I ran after the bird, getting hotter every minute, and when it landed in the middle of the road I persuaded it to go into a ditch where I caught it and returned it to some nearby water meadows.

Swan Round-Ups

I have already mentioned the 'Swan-Upping' on the Thames; however, the biggest round-up of the Mute Swan in recent years has been on the Fleet in July or August.

We have discovered recently that large numbers of non-breeding swans which normally live on the Somerset Levels make their way onto the Fleet during late June and early July before their moult, or flightless period. The reason is the vast quantity of marine eel grass which they can reach easily, without ever having to come on land during this six weeks annual danger period in their lives. If they do not wish to have anything to do with humans then they stay in the East Fleet away from the rest of the breeding birds at the west end of the Fleet. These 'incomers', as we call them, will be in company with practically all last year's surviving young from Abbotsbury with some from other areas. These numbers fluctuate considerably but have numbered over 600 to over 800 which have actually been caught, and several hundred rung or re-rung.

Some people might argue why bother the poor birds, and there is too much 'messing about' with wild life by humans anyway. I do have a lot of sympathy with people who feel like that. However, the Mute Swan is not adverse to human company and when caught will nearly always return to what it was doing prior to being caught, seemingly unconcerned. The Mute Swan cannot be identified except for one or two individuals which might have different distinguishing marks such as one of our birds which was killed by a fox in old age in 1983, who had a peculiar extension of the black area on her bill, but this is rare. So a ring number can give an identity or personality to that bird and the objects of ringing are there to see:
  (1) How long the bird lives
  (2) At what age it finds a mate
  (3) Does it keep the same nest site?
  (4) Does it keep the same mate? (Not always)
  (5) How many eggs it lays
  (6) The survival rate of its young
  (7) How long it lives
  (8) There are several rare blood group types and the whole genetic process can be followed.
We can now follow the life history of the great-grandparents, their successes in breeding etc., and this in the long run can only benefit the species. Another point about ringing Mute

Swan Round-Ups

Swans which has been of benefit is the highlighting of the lead poisoning problem back in the 'sixties. Yes, it has as usual taken us about twenty-five years to get round to the lead poisoning problem. Without rings, i.e. identification of individual swans, it would have been difficult in some cases to find out in which areas the birds had picked up the lead.

In the early stages I had reservations about blood samples being taken from the swans, but having seen some several hundred taken with the birds showing no signs of after-effects I no longer am concerned.

The first round-up we did in 1980, 823 birds were caught and only 10 got away. It is accomplished by gradually and carefully moving the birds to a prepared gently sloping site from the water's edge on land from a vast water area. This is accomplished with rowing boats and canoes making a circle gradually so as not to panic the birds, bearing in mind that the birds are in their moulting period as already mentioned. When the birds are on the land they do not panic and rush about but stand in the penned area with craned necks, i.e. being very curious about the whole process.

The first two round-ups had meant that the next day some of the swans were slightly reluctant to come on land at the nest site, but most had forgotten about the whole thing and two days afterwards all had been forgotten. The last round-up, 1984, all the swans had forgotten the next day. We do this once every two years with teams of people who deal with swans.

The Law

The Law

The law is quite specific and under the 'Wildlife and Countryside Act' of 1981 the 'wildness of mute swans' and their protection has been reinforced.

(1) It is illegal to interfere with the nesting of Mute Swans.

(2) It is illegal to take eggs.

(3) It is illegal to interfere with or harm the young.

(4) It is illegal to shoot Mute Swans unless you can prove that they are damaging your livelihood, and the onus is on the person concerned to prove that they have done everything in their power to try other ways of preventing that damage in the first place. Scientists and people working on *bona fide* studies have to be licensed by the Nature Conservancy Council (N.C.C.) to work on them.

(5) Any moving of birds must be done with the permission of the N.C.C.

Scientific Work

Although one of the most studied birds in Britain, there is still much to learn about the Mute Swan and to this end there are quite a number of studies taking place in the country by field workers who you may see from time to time putting rings on swans and juveniles. Practically all swans will have two rings, a coloured Darvic on the right leg below the ankle joint and the lettering or numbering is read upwards. On the left leg is a metal light very hard alloy ring which is a British Trust for Ornithology number which says 'Please inform the British Museum' and a number. These studies are carried out under the auspices of the Wildfowl Trust at Slimbridge, the Edward Grey Institute of Ornithology at Oxford, and the British Trust for Ornithology.

Rings

Lead Poisoning and Allied Problems

Lead Poisoning

There has been considerable talk about lead poisoning in the last few years. Much has been written, and there has been a lot of emotive talk by people both from the swans' side and the angling side, people who are not in possession of the full facts. Angling weights, both split shot size up to ledger weight size, have almost eliminated the Mute Swan from some areas in Great Britain, and places like parts of the Thames and the Avon at Stratford have been badly affected. There are several problems which I will enlarge upon in detail.

The Mute Swan's intake of food is either from the plants brought up from the bed of water, or grazed from alongside the river bank. Areas which are heavily fished, and where nylon line has been discarded along with split shot and hooks, means that swans will undoubtedly get caught up and separate lead shot that is discarded on the river bank will be ingested. This has resulted in many deaths as tons, yes tons, of lead are lost annually in this fashion. I quote from available authorities on sponsored lead shot pick-ups on stretches of river banks. The Mute Swan also is badly affected in some areas by taking in lead accidentally with grit from the bed of the river, canal or lake.

To digest its food it has a largish muscular part near its stomach called a gizzard. The point of taking in grit is this: they have no teeth so the food passes into the gizzard which acts like a coffee grinder, and the food is ground down by the grit. The lead shot is also ground down at the same time and passes into the bird's system. The following then happens: the bird cannot absorb food and the food is left in the gizzard. Meanwhile the lead affects the nervous system, causing loss of control, the bill loses its colour, it can no longer hold up its head which lies along its back. If it has only received two or three shot its flying ability has been impaired and it is more likely to fly into power lines. To leave hooks on nylon line on the river bank means that many things apart from swans are at risk. Now, to be fair to some river anglers, they do not discard nylon line, hooks or lead shot, but having been an

Gizzard

ardent angler for many years I do know what can happen accidentally. Sometimes when fishing with very light tackle hooks can get caught round 'snags' or plants in the water. Nylon these days is very fine and all anglers are using very fine terminal tackle, i.e. the last few feet of tackle which has swivels, lead shot and hooks on it. The hooks or lead shot weights are caught in the weed and the only way to get it loose is to break the tackle. There is hope, through many of the good clubs who are now insisting on the new alternatives to lead shot being used by their members, that things will improve.

In some areas there is considerable resistance to using the new alternatives, which are largely being condemned out of hand without giving them a fair trial. I have seen the best of these alternatives and they are far superior to lead, very versatile, opening up new ideas in fishing, and where they have been used in fishing competitions the people using them are winning competitions. As to hooks we have been called to many incidents in recent years involving Mute Swans, but we also often find other diving birds such as Cormorants with sea fishing tackle bound round them, causing them to starve to death. The latest case I dealt with myself was a call to West Bay, Dorset, by the Harbour Master's office, where I found a swan unable to move with five mackerel hooks in its body, feet and wings. We managed to release him on the river at West Bay unharmed. This incident was probably the end result of an angler who bought a brand new carbon fibre rod and who went into a local hostelry at Abbotsbury for a drink before fishing off Abbotsbury beach. He cast out and went to sleep. He was awakened by the sound of a screaming reel and probably thinking he had the fish of a lifetime he jumped up to see two hundred pounds worth of rod and Swedish reel disappearing out to sea attached to a swan, where it was lost. If this angler was bottom fishing and not feathering for mackerel we still probably have the swan which became enmeshed in his hooks, as we found a one-legged swan in our last round-up. I do not know whether this bird can fly but he can certainly swim perfectly all right; as already mentioned Mute Swans spend a lot of their time swimming with one leg up anyway.

We do not hear much about other waterfowl which are dying from picking up lead shot which has either been spilt from lead shot dispensers or from cartridges, probably the swans' story has overshadowed it, but one only tiny lead shot will kill a Mallard, seven will kill a swan, as will one large ledger weight. We have the largest regular wintering flock of Mute Swans in the British Isles and I have only seen one or two swans in ten years with this lead poisoning problem, and they were incomers. We, in common with other wildlife, all have lead in very small quantities in our systems but, of course, there is an unacceptable level. We have never permitted angling in the Fleet, the eight mile stretch of water behind the Chesil Bank.

In 1980 we had 101 pairs of swans nesting in our colony and I carefully collected eggshell from many nests, when nesting was finished, and put this in a plastic bag along with the ring numbers of the pairs. This went to the Edward Grey Institute of Ornithology at Oxford and our colony of swans became the 'control' to work out sub-lethal and lethal doses of lead in swans in the rest of the country, our birds having less lead in their systems than other swans analysed. Independent scientists, nothing to do with Bird Conservation groups, now have the full facts regarding mortality caused by lead poisoning and it seems that in areas which are heavily fished for coarse fish, i.e. not trout or salmon, then lead poisoning is a problem. But elsewhere the Mute Swan is holding his own. It has been estimated that approximately 3,000 swans in the British population are dying annually from lead poisoning and allied causes. Let us hope sense prevails and that the new alternatives are adopted more widely before it becomes illegal to use lead for fishing, but it would make sense if the alternatives to lead were cheaper not more expensive.

Juveniles Dispersing

Juveniles have to find a new place on water where there is enough food when they have been driven off by the parents. This of course is very difficult as most good places are already filled by other adults. Juveniles also probably require more food than the adults as they not only have the large body weight to maintain but also are still developing. Juveniles when eating on grass in captivity especially on a lawn, often develop a lump under the lower mandible. This is a 'grass ball' which they cannot get rid of themselves, but it can easily be removed by opening the bill and hooking it out with one's finger. For the rest of the food, wheat in the water or maize and stale wholemeal bread well soaked. Not white bread, as this can kill swans if they receive too much, so it is better not to give them any at all. Grass cuttings with clover is a favourite especially if spread on the water. (Make sure that no pesticides, weedkillers, etc. have been used on the grass where the cuttings are obtained.) Maize can be used for feeding purposes but it is expensive and has not such a high protein content as wheat. They are not fond of barley but will eat it if nothing else is available.

Grass Ball

Feeding in Captivity

Diseases

Diseases

Avian botulism

Unfortunately until recently little was known about some of the causes of early deaths. However, the drought of 1976 brought a team of people visiting all areas with heavy concentration of birds on them. Avian botulism type C was rife that year owing to the lack of water to wash away the problem. Strangely enough, in many areas of Great Britain human botulism was found, but only in a few places was avian botulism discovered.

Avian tuberculosis

Avian tuberculosis is endemic in our ground at Abbotsbury, although the site is free of swans from September to February each year, and washed by the elements, sea water etc. Some years it takes a fair toll of our young cygnets, but I believe that the old Jeyes Fluid works wonders watered into the ground in our cygnet rearing pens before they are brought into use.

Pulmonary pneumonia

This is a real killer during very cold wet weather. Last winter, 1984/85, although very hard, with three-quarters of our eight mile stretch of salt water frozen right over, had been a good year for survival, whereas the relatively mild winters of 1981/82 and 1982/83 saw great losses, especially in the juvenile population, owing to food shortages. Starving swans fall very quickly prey to such things as pneumonia, but if you find a bird, even if it is extremely thin and listless, it can be saved by feeding up; but of course pneumonia is a difficult problem.

Aspergillosis

This is a fungus which affects the respiratory system and lungs, and causes death.

Feather-lice – mallophaga, and feather-mite – sarcoptiformes

Swans have their own particular feather-lice and feather-mite, which increase in number when the bird is out of condition.

Worms: Round-worm – nematodes, and tapeworm – cestodes

Worms can debilitate considerably, in fact may be a contributing factor to a fairly low survival rate in young birds. If they are already infested, they are fighting a losing battle. I believe that juvenile swans have to take in more food per body weight than adults, to survive until twelve months old.

Further Reading

Further Reading

One of the best books on the Mute Swan is 'The Swans' by Sir Peter Scott and the Wildfowl Trust, published by Michael Joseph, 1972, but I believe this is out of print at present.

One which is rather more scientific is 'Handbook of the Birds of Europe, the Middle East and North Africa, The Birds of the Western Palearctic', Chief Editor Stanley Cramp, published by the Oxford University Press, 1977. This covers the geese as well as the swans and is an R.S.P.B. book.

The history of swan marks etc. is very well covered by 'The Mute Swan in England' by N. F. Ticehurst. It is published by Cleaver-Hume, 1957, and although it may be out of print some libraries may have a copy. It delves into the history of the Mute Swan in Britain and swan marks.

Uses to which Swans have been put in the past

(1) Fresh meat supply, for Feast days, Banquets, etc.
(2) Dead swans were skinned and the skins sewn together to make swan 'quilts'.
(3) Down used in pillows and swansdown quilts.
(4) Feathers used in calligraphy. The primary feathers, large eighteen inch long feathers on the end of wings, are called quills. Lloyds Register in London still use quills from our swans to write in the Loss Book, a book which has existed since the eighteenth century, in which Lloyds record every ship registered with them when it sinks or is lost. I would point out here that these primaries, or quills, are shed naturally during the moult.
(5) Paddles, i.e. feet, were sometimes used to make tobacco pouches, when deboned and sewn together.
(6) Pin feathers, used by clockmakers for oiling clocks. These are stiff small feathers, two in each wing on the leading edge, near the large primaries.
(7) The latest and newest information on swan bones used in mediaeval times to make a musical instrument, a flute, is not quite complete as I am awaiting a reply from America. We do know that the swan wing bone flute was made before 1050, and was found in a castle in Germany.
(8) A primary, or quill, feather, is used by beekeepers to carefully 'comb' bees from the honey comb. The stiffness of a primary in a swan is apparently exactly right for this purpose. Black or dark feathers are not advisable as they upset the bees.

Fossil bones of *Cygnus olor* have been discovered from late Ice Age – Roman times.

Collective Names

Terms Used to Denote a Quantity of Swans Together

'A Game of Swans', refers to the days when they were used as a food source.

'A Herd', a quantity of managed swans on the land, consequently the term –

'A Swanherd'. These two terms are today only applicable to Abbotsbury.

'A Flight', a quantity of swans flying together.

'A Fleet', a quantity of swans on the water.

Acknowledgements

My wife, Yvonne, for encouragement.

Mrs. Doreen E. Daltry, for sorting out and typing the script.

Mr. C. B. Berry, for lending me the painting 'Morning Flight'.

Mr. Brian Harding, for the use of his photograph 'The Pied Piper'.

And finally, but not least, Mr. Philip Snowden, for editing and many points in helping me put this together.

John Fair

Index